"Get ready for a delightful 25-day journey through the month of December, one that's filled with fun, adventure, creativity, and excitement as your children discover the wonders of Christ's birth. Carol Garborg has a heartfelt, hands-on, Jesus-focused, imaginative, instructive, easy to understand, joy-filled way of helping children discover who Jesus is and why He came. Her animated, syncopated style will help children discover such priceless truths as…

- The God of the mountain is also the God of the minnow!
- The God of then is the God of now!
- Peace is not a something but a Someone!"

ROY LESSIN

THE
FAMILY
BOOK OF
ADVENT

CAROL GARBORG

25 **Stories & Activities** to Celebrate
the Meaning of **Christmas**

summerside
PRESS

Summerside Press™
Minneapolis, MN 55378
www.summersidepress.com

The Family Book of Advent: 25 Stories & Activities to Celebrate the Meaning of Christmas

© 2012 by Carol Garborg

ISBN 978-1-60936-541-7

Unless otherwise indicated, all Scripture quotations are taken from The Holy Bible, New International Version®, NIV®. Copyright © 1973, 1978, 1984 by Biblica, Inc.™ Used by permission of Zondervan. All rights reserved worldwide. Other Scripture references are from the following sources: The New King James Version (NKJV). Copyright © 1982 by Thomas Nelson, Inc. Used by permission. The Holy Bible, New Living Translation (NLT), copyright 1996, 2004. Used by permission of Tyndale House Publishers, Inc., Wheaton, Illinois. The New American Standard Bible® (NASB), Copyright © 1960, 1962, 1963, 1968, 1971, 1972, 1973, 1975, 1977, 1995 by The Lockman Foundation. Used by permission.

Cover and interior design by Thinkpen Design | www.thinkpendesign.com

Any Internet addresses (website, blog, etc.) printed in this book are offered as a resource. They are not intended in any way to be or imply an endorsement by Summerside Press, nor does Summerside Press vouch for the content of these sites for the life of this book.

Stock or custom editions of Summerside Press titles may be purchased in bulk for educational, business, ministry, fundraising, or sales promotional use. For information, please e-mail specialmarkets@summersidepress.com.

Summerside Press™ is an inspirational publisher offering fresh, irresistible books to uplift the heart and engage the mind.

Printed in China.

**DEDICATED
TO MY FAMILY**

With special thanks to…

Dad and Mom, Kjell and Davis, John and Amy Haley, Tony and Jeanne Hedrick, and Noemi Hedrick for your prayer support.

To the moms, dads, and kids who gave me feedback about the crafts, stories, and activities in this book— Dave, Janet, Elijah, Ezekiel, Noah, and Phoebe Horsman; Kristi, Giovanna, and Luana Fonseca; Matt, Noemi, and Adriah Hedrick; Cate and Avery Mezyk; Kim and Chase Bixel; Deirdre, Evan, and Ainsley Thompson; Laurie Dahlen; Lisa Garborg; Erin, Elijah, and Mia Haase.

To Eva Poppen who helped me with the research for this book.

To Jason Rovenstine and Marilyn Jansen at Summerside Press for their patience, creativity, and heart for family.

CONTENTS

The Advent

COUNTDOWN TO CHRISTMAS

takes **25** DAYS.

To finish right on

Jesus' birthday,

start your

FAMILY ADVENT ADVENTURE

on

December 1.

To be prepared for all of these adventures,
see the Supply List on page 130.

"WHEN WILL IT BE CHRISTMAS?"

A soggy piece of pumpkin pie slumps toward the bottom of the kitchen sink. Turkey leftovers slouch inside a Ziploc bag. The final football game of the day winds down as the players huddle around the ball, and Thanksgiving lumbers into hibernation.

This sleepy picture belies the next day's plunge into a four-week frenzy. Buy the tree. Untangle lights. Hang the stockings. Bake cookies. (Scratch that.) Run to the bakery. Address envelopes, and answer over and over the question that pulses with excitement, "Dad...Mom...Mommy! When will it be Christmas?"

Our children can plunge us into insanity with their wide-eyed wanting and pleading. How we respond to their excitement communicates more about Christmas than any carefully crafted sermon. Is Christmas when joy came into the world or is it the time when Mom is always tense and Dad is always busy?

When Jesus told us to become like little children, He spoke of their humility and faith. But I believe He hinted at something else—joy. The Scriptures are full of terms of celebration. The people shout for joy (Psalm 33:3). The mountains sing;

the rivers clap (Psalm 98:8). And Jesus Himself encouraged joy (John 17:13).

One day, moms and dads brought their children to Jesus. Imagine little children clustered around Jesus, crawling on His lap and tugging at His arm.

"Hello, Mr. Jesus."

"Did you really make dinner for five thousand people?"

"Why did you spit in the dirt and make mud? My mom says I'm not supposed to spit."

"Can't you see Jesus is busy?" said the disciples. "Shoo. Not now."

Jesus, however, surprised everyone and gave the children joy. "Let the little children come to Me. Don't keep them away. Come on!"

So often our reaction to our children's excitement parallels the disciples'. When our children burst into the kitchen, arms wiggling, feet dancing, and they blurt out, "Mom, can I pleeease…." or "When can we bake cookies?" we say, "I'll think about it." "Maybe later." "Just be patient." "I'm busy now." Slowly the arms stop wiggling, the feet become still, and the bubbling slows to a simmer. Inadvertently, we've taken away a little bit of their joy.

What if, instead of reining in our kids, we jumped into their joy? What if we used their sense of anticipation to teach them about Christmas?

The Family Book of Advent will give your family practical ways to encourage your children's excitement while exploring the many lessons packed into the Christmas story. You'll find concrete lessons on prayer, thankfulness, and creation, but the theme of joy will pop up more than any other theme. Why? Because Advent means "coming," and with the coming of any long-awaited special someone comes loads of excitement and anticipation. The people of Israel anticipated Christ's coming for two thousand years, and we can anticipate the celebration of His birth now.

The next time you hear the question for the thousandth time, "When will it be Christmas?" match your children's enthusiasm and direct it into an opportunity to explore the best story ever told.

On Day 1, you'll create a wreath designed to emphasize the names of Jesus. As you read each devotional, look for any names of Jesus tucked into the Scripture verses in italics. The words "Name Alert" mean you'll find one name, sometimes more. Don't see "Name Alert"? That means there are no names that day.

When you discover a name of Jesus, write that name on an ornament, decorate around it, and add it to your wreath. By the end of the twenty-five days, your wreath will be decorated with fifteen ornaments. (Some names will be used more than once.)

Day	Title	Name for Ornament
Day 1	**HE'S COMING!**	*King*
Day 3	**A REAL PERSON**	*Immanuel*
Day 5	**INSIDE OUT**	*Son of the Most High*
Day 6	**A GREAT NAME**	*Jesus*
Day 10	**A PARENT TO LOVE ME**	*Jesus*
Day 12	**HAPPY BIRTHDAY, JESUS!**	*Wonderful Counselor, Mighty God, Everlasting Father, Prince of Peace*
Day 14	**SCARED SHEPHERDS**	*Savior, Christ the Lord*
Day 17	**FOLLOW THE STAR**	*King of the Jews*
Day 18	**JUST ONE KING**	*Christ*
Day 25	**COMING—AGAIN!**	*Lord of Lords, King of Kings*

HOPE

"When someone has hope, they have a little excited face and a little worried face. They're not sure, but they're hoping."

MIA, 8

HIGHLIGHTING HOPE

When we think of hope, we often think of the I-hope-it-happens-but-I'm-not-sure-it-will kind of hope. Maybe it'll happen; maybe it won't. The hope that the people of Israel experienced was a solid expectation that God would keep His promise and send His Son. It was an I-know-it-will-happen-it's-just-a-matter-of-when hope.

In his name the nations will put their hope.
MATTHEW 12:21

The hope we have in Christ is an absolute certainty.... With Him nothing is left to chance. Everything He promised He will deliver.
BILLY GRAHAM

ADVENT FAMILY ACTIVITY

Evergreen branches are used to symbolize God's never-ending faithfulness. Because God is faithful, we can have hope. Place evergreen boughs on a mantel or table. Set a candle, the HOPE candle, among the boughs. Remember that God was faithful in keeping His promise to send Jesus.

HOPE FOR PARENTS
HEAVEN'S VIEW

Thousands of years after Eve's tempter slithered his way into Eden, God's redemption plan was finally about to begin. All the heavenly host gathered around to watch the angel Gabriel deliver his message to Zechariah.

"Your wife, Elizabeth, will have a son," Gabriel announced to Zechariah. "He will prepare the way for the coming Lord."

His message delivered, I imagine Gabriel fell silent while angels and saints held their breath, awaiting Zechariah's response.

Zechariah straightened. He cleared his throat. "How can I be sure of this? After all, I'm really old, and my wife is old too."

The angels covered their eyes in embarrassment. Abraham shook his head. Elijah simply fumed.

"Are you kidding me?" said the angel Michael. He threw his wings up in frustration.

So often as parents we react like Zechariah. We speak from our puny perspective of what we see and know. "How will we ever afford health insurance, God?" Or, "My five-year-old will never learn self-control. What am I going to do?" We cram God into the confines of our imaginations. We define what He can do by the size of our tiny worlds.

As you read through the Christmas story, ask God to stretch your faith and fill your heart with hope—hope in who God is and what He'll do in your family this Christmas season. He longs for you to believe in His greatness and to see life from His perspective instead of from your own.

Have faith—and hope!

❄ DAY 1 ❄
HE'S COMING!

People wait for a King to come. LUKE 2:25, 38

:: **EXPLORE BEFORE** ::

SUPPLIES: A clear plastic bottle of soda (This can be messy. Consider doing the activity in a laundry room, garage, or outside)

Before starting the devotional whisper to your child, "Guess what? It's coming." Don't tell him what's coming. Build his anticipation by smiling and saying from time to time, "Guess what? It's coming!" When he begs to know what, say, "Soon. Real soon."

When he can't bear the suspense any longer, hand him the bottle of soda. Then read the story.

Years ago, the people of Israel waited for the Messiah, a King who would save them. You've been waiting for a few minutes. The people of Israel waited for hundreds of years.

Your King is coming to you; He is just and having salvation (Zechariah 9:9 NKJV).

"When is He coming?" asked the moms.

"I hope He comes soon," said the dads.

"We can't wait!" said all the boys and the girls.

And so they waited. (*Have your child shake the bottle and watch what happens to the bubbles inside.*) And they waited. (*Shake the bottle harder and watch the bubbles.*) And they waited. (*Shake the bottle as hard as you can.*)

They waited until they were bursting inside. One day God said, "Guess what? It's time. The King is on His way!" (*Take the cap off and let the foam bubble over.*)

After hundreds of years, the King was coming! A King who would bring hope, joy, peace, light, and love to the world.

At Christmastime, you celebrate the coming of this King—Jesus. As you read the Christmas story from beginning to end during the next twenty-four days, you'll count down the days to Christmas— the day of Jesus' coming.

So what's coming? Christmas is coming!

Name Alert

__   __   __   __

:: ADVENT ADVENTURE: NAMES OF JESUS WREATH ::

During the next twenty-four days, use this wreath to emphasize the names of Jesus. Add an ornament to the wreath each time you find a name of Jesus within the italicized Scripture verse(s) each day.

SUPPLIES: A wreath, 15 small plain ball ornaments, permanent markers
(consider gold or silver to go with the holiday theme)

DIRECTIONS:
- Buy a small wreath or create your own by wrapping ribbon around a simple foam wreath or attaching garland to a wire wreath frame. (Go to The Family Book of Advent link under www.faithfamilystyle.com for video instructions.)
- Every time you hear a name of Jesus in the story for the day, use the marker to write that name on the ball ornament.
- Decorate the ornament with stripes, polka dots, squiggles, or swirls.
- Hang the ornament on the wreath.

By the end of 25 days, you'll have a beautiful handcrafted wreath that illustrates the meaning of Christmas.

Where does a circle start? Where does it end?

God has no beginning and no end, just like a circle, the shape of your wreath. He always was and always will be; He never stops being God. Whenever you see your wreath, remember that God is always _____ (fill in the blank with the name on the ornaments, e.g., King).

PRAYER TO SHARE

Dear God, I'm so excited for Christmas I could burst. Thank You for sending Jesus. I can't wait to celebrate His birthday. Amen.

CHRISTMAS COUNTDOWN

It's coming! It's coming!
Christmas is coming!
Only ___ more days until Christmas!

❄ DAY 2 ❄
I PROMISE

God gives Ahaz a sign. ISAIAH 7:1–14

King Ahaz was scared. His knees knocked together. His arms trembled. The hearts of the king and all his people shook like the trees of a forest whipped around by the wind.

Two armies marched down the road to attack King Ahaz and his city. Two armies that had ruined cities and captured prisoners.

Hup, two, three, four.

Hup, two, three, four.

What am I going to do? thought King Ahaz.

The king turned and saw Isaiah and his son standing next to him.

"I have a message from God," Isaiah the prophet said, "God says… *Be careful, keep calm and don't be afraid* (Isaiah 7:4).

"The two kings and their armies won't destroy you or your city. This is how you'll know what I'm saying is true:

"*The Lord himself will give you a sign: The virgin will be with child and will give birth to a son*" (v. 14).

Still King Ahaz trembled. He didn't keep calm, and he was very afraid. The two armies seemed so big; God seemed so far away. *Will I really win?* thought King Ahaz. *Will God help me like He promised?* King Ahaz didn't think so, and he asked another king, King Tiglath-Pileser, to help him instead.

How do you think God felt when King Ahaz asked someone else for help?

Do you think God keeps His promises? All of the time?

God *does* keep all His promises. If He says something, you can believe it's true. Always true. Just like He keeps His promises, He asks you to keep yours. When you say you'll do something, do it. If you can't do something, don't make a promise that you will. God is faithful to keep all His promises. Be faithful to keep all of yours.

:: ADVENT ADVENTURE: PICTURE PROMISE POCKET ::

SUPPLIES: small plain gift bag, four pieces of paper that will fit inside the bag, glue stick, markers

DIRECTIONS:

- Write "Promise Pocket" on the outside of the gift bag.
- On each of the four pieces of paper, draw a picture of one of the following: an angel, any kind of food, a heart, a snowman.
- Under each picture write the corresponding phrase: 1. God tells His ANGELS to take care of you (Psalm 91:11). 2. God feeds the birds of the air; He'll give you FOOD too (Matthew 6:26). 3. Nothing can separate you from God's LOVE (Romans 8:38-39). 4. God forgives our sins and makes us white like SNOW.
- Place the four promises inside the pocket and hang on a doorknob.

PARENT TIP: *Pairing a picture with a verse makes Scripture learning easy. It introduces something unfamiliar (a verse) by associating it with something familiar (a picture).*

I WONDER

I WONDER

Why does it hurt people's feelings when
someone breaks a promise?

PRAYER TO SHARE

Dear God, You keep all Your promises. You always do what
You say. Help me keep my promises like You do. Amen.

CHRISTMAS COUNTDOWN

It's coming! It's coming!
Christmas is coming!
Only ___ more days until Christmas!

❄ DAY 3 ❄
A REAL PERSON

God would become a human being. ISAIAH 7:14

:: **EXPLORE BEFORE** ::

Parents, have your child call a friend or a grandparent on the phone and tell them about what he did yesterday ("Guess what I did yesterday? I..."), what he'll do tomorrow ("Guess what I'm doing tomorrow? I..."), or about a best friend ("I have a best friend. I really like her because..."). After he's said good-bye, ask him the questions below.

- Would you rather talk to someone on the phone or be with her/him? Why?
- What can you do with someone on the phone? *Talk with her.*
- What can you do when that person's with you? *Play hide-and-seek or make crafts.*

When a friend is sitting next to you, she can do what you do, like taste your chocolate birthday cake and whack a piñata. Your friend doesn't just hear about your party; she experiences it too.

God wanted to be *with* people and do what they do. He didn't want to just talk about it. He wanted to experience it. So He made a promise to come and live on earth.

> *The Lord himself will give you a sign: The virgin will be with child and will give birth to a son, and will call him Immanuel* (Isaiah 7:14).

Immanuel means "God with us." God promised someday He would leave His heaven world to live in our earth world. God would become a burping baby, a sweaty boy, a working man. He'd eat and laugh and cry just like you and me. What a promise!

On Christmas Day Jesus came into the world as a baby, just like God promised. Because He did, He knows what it's like to…

- taste what we taste—salty, sour, bitter, and sweet
- smell what we smell—stinky feet and freshly baked bread
- hear what we hear—clucking chickens and the sloshing blue sea
- see what we see—flickering fireflies and 'round-the-sky rainbows
- feel what we feel—bumblebee stings and grandma's warm hugs

What do *you* taste, smell, hear, and see?

What do *you* feel, both inside and out?

Jesus knows what it's like to be a kid and a grown-up too. He understands because He's Immanuel, God who came to be *with* us—not a God who's far away from us (John 1:14). So the next time you're bursting with joy or frustrated because you don't think anyone understands, remember *Jesus* knows and He understands. He was a real person like you and me.

:: **ADVENT ADVENTURE: SHADOWS** ::

SUPPLIES: Lamp or flashlight, a plain wall, and—you!

DIRECTIONS:

- Turn the lamp on and shine it toward the wall.
- Place your hand between the lamp and the wall to make shadows.
- Try making different shapes on the wall using your hand.
- What happens when your hand moves up? Down?

Whatever you do, your shadow does too. Because Jesus, Immanuel, lived with us, He understands what it's like to do what you do, throw a pitch, twirl around, and climb into bed at night.

Name Alert

— — — — — — E L

I WONDER

What would it be like to live in heaven? What would it be like to leave heaven and come down to earth?

PRAYER TO SHARE

Dear God, no one knows me like You do. I can talk to You anywhere about anything and You understand. You know what it's like to be me. Amen.

CHRISTMAS COUNTDOWN

It's coming! It's coming!
Christmas is coming!
Only ___ more days until Christmas!

❊ DAY 4 ❊
HAPPY TO ANSWER

Zechariah and Elizabeth pray for a son. LUKE 1:5–25

Have you ever begged your mom or dad, "Please can I have a sleepover?" or "Please can I stay up late?" What do you do if they say yes? Jump up and down? Holler and shout *Yippee!* and *Hurray!*?

For many years Zechariah and Elizabeth had asked God, "Please, God, give us a son." Elizabeth wanted a little baby to hold and cuddle, someone who would call her Mom. Zechariah wanted a boy who'd grow up to be like him, a priest in God's temple. But both Zechariah and Elizabeth were now old, past the time for having babies. God still hadn't answered their prayers.

One day when Zechariah was in the temple, a shining angel appeared.

The angel said to him: "Do not be afraid, Zechariah; your prayer has been heard. Your wife Elizabeth will bear you a son, and you are to give him the name John. He will be a joy and delight to you" (Luke 1:13–15).

God said yes! He was going to give Zechariah and Elizabeth a son, someone who'd prepare the way for Jesus!

What do you think Zechariah did when God said yes? Jump up and down? Holler and shout *Yippee!* and *Hurray!*?

Zechariah stared at that angel and said, "Hmm, how do I know this is true? After all, I am an old man and my wife is old too."

The angel frowned and said,

> Now you will be silent and not able to speak until the day this happens, because you did not believe my words (Luke 1:20).

Zechariah walked out of the temple and couldn't say a word. He opened his mouth and nothing came out.

God always answers prayers. When He does, He can sound a lot like your mom or dad. He may say, "I don't think so," or "Sure." Or, "Let me think about it," or "I think you can wait."

No matter what His answer, God always hears the prayers of those who love and obey Him. When you pray, God is listening. He might say "yes." He might say "no." He might say "maybe" or "wait a little while." Don't be like Zechariah; expect God to answer because He *will*!

:: Advent Adventure: Smelly Prayers ::

SUPPLIES: Before beginning this adventure with your child, gather various items that have either a pleasant or an unpleasant smell. Keep them out of sight until you're ready to begin. Some ideas: cinnamon, perfume, vinegar, a dirty sock, pine needles, a candle.

DIRECTIONS:
- Close your eyes.
- Smell each item and decide whether you like it or not.
- Place the "like-its" in one pile and the "don't-like-its" in another.
- When you're done, open your eyes.

God says the prayers of those who love Him are like incense (Revelation 5:8). Incense in the Bible was wonderful perfume that filled the air. When you pray, it smells good to God. He puts your prayer in His "like-it" pile.

I WONDER

Why is God happy when I pray to Him?

PRAYER TO SHARE

Dear God, thank You for answering my prayers.
When I pray, I know You're listening. Amen.

CHRISTMAS COUNTDOWN

It's coming! It's coming!
Christmas is coming!
Only ___ more days until Christmas!

❄ DAY 5 ❄
INSIDE OUT

The angel Gabriel visits Mary. LUKE 1:26–38

:: EXPLORE BEFORE ::

Play a quick game of "Eeny meeny miny moe" to see who will snuggle with Mom, sit next to Dad, choose a snack, etc.
Eeny meeny miny moe.
Catch a tiger by the toe.
If he hollers let him go.
Eeny meeny miny moe.
My mother told me to pick the very best one
And that is you!

"Pick me, pick me! Please pick me." We all want to be picked—to go first, to help the teacher, to be on a baseball team.

God had to pick someone to be the mother of Jesus. Who would He choose? Maybe He'd choose a woman with _____ (*parents, please fill in the blank with what your child would consider beautiful, e.g., long, dark, curly hair*) or _____ (*e.g., big blue/green eyes).* Maybe He'd choose someone famous, a princess, or someone with heaps of money.

God spied the perfect mother for Jesus tucked in a tiny town called Nazareth. A poor girl named Mary was sweeping her kitchen floor.

"Gabriel," God said to His top angel, "tell Mary I pick her to be the mother of Jesus."

Off the angel Gabriel flew. He stopped at Mary's door and said…

> *"Greetings, you who are highly favored! The Lord is with you…. You will be with child and give birth to a son…. He will be great and will be called the Son of the Most High."*
>
> *"How will this be," Mary asked the angel, "since I am a virgin?" [Virgins can't have babies.]*
>
> *The angel answered, "The Holy Spirit will come upon you…. Nothing is impossible with God."*
>
> *"I am the Lord's servant," Mary answered. "May it be to me as you have said"* (Luke 1:28–38).

God looked at Mary's heart and liked what He saw (1 Samuel 16:7). She was young and poor and from an unimportant town, but she believed that nothing was impossible for God. Mary didn't have money or fame, but she had what God wanted—a believing heart.

When you pick someone to be on your side or to come over and play, who do you pick? Someone with a big swimming pool or who owns mountains of toys? Someone who has pretty clothes or can hit deep into right field? Remember how God picked Mary. He didn't look at the outside; He looked on the inside and saw her heart.

Name Alert

— — —

of the

— — — —   — — — —

What's one thing that *is* impossible for
God to do? (See Hebrews 6:18.)

PRAYER TO SHARE

Dear God, I want to be like You
and look on the inside. Amen.

CHRISTMAS COUNTDOWN

It's coming! It's coming!
Christmas is coming!
Only ___ more days until Christmas!

❄ DAY 6 ❄
A GREAT NAME

The angel tells Mary to name the baby "Jesus." LUKE 1:31

Once upon a time there was a man surrounded by enemies trying to attack him. "Lord, help me!" the man yelled. "Please save me!"

In heaven, God heard his cry. The earth trembled. The mountains shook. God split the heavens and soared down, like an eagle cuts through the sky. Bolts of lightning crackled. Thunder exploded and hailstones fell. God shot His arrows and the enemies scattered.

Then God reached down and rescued the man. He saved him from his enemies and put him in a safe place. (Based on Psalm 18.)

Wouldn't it be nice to know you could call for help and someone would always save you?

"Help, I'm afraid. Can you please keep me safe?"

"Help, I'm lonely. Can you please give me a friend?"

There is one name you can always call on for help—Jesus. When the angel visited Mary, he said…

> *"You will be with child and give birth to a son, and you*
> *are to give him the name Jesus"* (Luke 1:31).

"Jesus" means Savior or Rescuer. When you call His name, He saves you—from being afraid, from being angry, and from any enemies.

Best of all, He saves you from the ugliness of sin. He washes you clean and makes your heart white like snow. If you're ever in trouble and need help, or if you need forgiveness, just call His name—Jesus!

:: ADVENT ADVENTURE: NAMES OF JESUS WORD ART (OPT. 1) ::

SUPPLIES: Computer, paper, color printer

DIRECTIONS:

- Go to www.wordle.net and click Create.
- Type in any text that includes the name of Jesus. For example, you might type, "The name of Jesus gives life. The name of Jesus has power. The name of Jesus is above every other name." (Note: the more frequently a word occurs, the larger it appears in the final product.)
- Click Go and see the design.
- Change the font and color if you want.
- Print and display.

:: ADVENT ADVENTURE: SALTY SNOW SCENE (OPT. 2) ::

Create a snow scene to remind you that the power of Jesus' name can make you white like snow. (See Isaiah 1:18.)

SUPPLIES: 2 c. sea salt, ½ c. water, aluminum foil, 8"x10" piece of cardboard, decorative pieces (e.g., mini pinecones, Lego people)

DIRECTIONS:

- Cover the cardboard with foil.
- Crunch up foil in the shape of rocks, etc., to add dimension to your scene.
- Set these shapes on the cardboard.
- Mix the water, tablespoon by tablespoon, into the salt.
- Drop, plop, glop, and press the salt over your scene, covering everything.
- Arrange decorative pieces (e.g., pinecones, Lego people).
- Set aside until dry.

:: **ADVENT ADVENTURE: BLOCK LETTERS (OPT. 3)** ::

SUPPLIES: paper, markers

DIRECTIONS:

- Draw the letters J-E-S-U-S in large block letters.
- Have your child use markers to fill them in with different shapes in different colors (e.g., triangles, circles, squares, diamonds).
- As your child colors ask, "When would be a time when you would call for Jesus?"

Name Alert

— — — — —

I WONDER

If all the people in the world asked for help at
the same time, could Jesus help them all?

PRAYER TO SHARE

Dear God, I need help with _____ (e.g.,
my math). My help comes from You, the One who made
heaven and earth. Amen. (Based on Psalm 121:2.)

A Prayer for Forgiveness—Dear Jesus, thank You for coming
to earth to save me from sin. Thank You for dying on the
cross. Please take away my sin and give me new life. Amen.

CHRISTMAS COUNTDOWN

It's coming! It's coming!
Christmas is coming!
Only ___ more days until Christmas!

SECTION 2

PEACE

"Peace is when you calm down. You kind of stop going 'Mama, I want to go sledding,' and you take a deep breath and count to ten and breathe again."

DELANEY, 6

HIGHLIGHTING PEACE

Any plans for peace and harmony and unity have to
include Jesus. Peace is not a something but a Someone.
Without Jesus there can no more be peace than
there can be chocolate cake without chocolate.

The government will be on his shoulders. And
he will be called…Prince of Peace.

ISAIAH 9:6

God cannot give us a happiness and peace apart
from Himself, because it is not there.

C. S. LEWIS

ADVENT FAMILY ACTIVITY

Add a second candle, the PEACE candle, and some holly to the
first candle and your evergreen boughs. Holly reminds us of why
Jesus came into the world—to die for our sins. The prickly holly
leaves symbolize the crown of thorns that would be placed on Jesus'
head. Remember God's faithfulness to send Jesus, the Prince of
Peace, so we could have peace with God.

PEACE FOR PARENTS
TOUGH TOPICS

"Mom, what's a virgin?"
"Why did Herod kill the babies?"

A few unexpected prickles poke out from in between the wonder and beauty of Christmas, tough subjects parents typically step around and walk past as quickly as they can. Whether the topic is the Virgin Mary or something unrelated to Christmas, here are a few simple tips to keep in mind before children and tough topics collide.

Prepare for tough topics by building on natural opportunities. During a visit to the zoo, I noticed two snapping turtles stacked on top of each other. "That's how grown-up turtles make baby turtles," I said to my six-year-old son, Davis.

"Okay," Davis said and then dashed off to check out the hippopotamus. Despite his cursory response, I knew I'd laid a foundation for future talks about sex. By snatching natural openings, talking about any sensitive topic can unfold over time. Rather than a big event, discussion becomes a small step in a direction you've already been going.

Turn a question around and ask one of your own. Ask, "What do you think?" Your child's response will give you a peek into her thinking, and you can use that information to create your answer. Your five-year-old may have asked, "How are babies born?" but only meant, "How do babies get out?"

Be cautious about explaining the whys.

Even for adults, the "why" question nags more than any other. "Why didn't God warn *all* the families in Bethlehem?" "Why did she lose her job, Lord?"

The truth is, few people know the reason why things happen. Even if they did, that reason might not satisfy, especially if they are hurting.

What we *do* know is God is love (1 John 4:8). Rather than interpreting what you do know in light of what you don't, interpret what you don't know in light of what you do—God is love. Instead of trying to answer "why" questions, point your child to God's character. God is love, and He has reasons we don't know yet.

❄ DAY 7 ❄
JUMP FOR JOY

Mary visits Elizabeth. LUKE 1:39–45

:: PARENT PREP ::

SUPPLIES: A deflated balloon

You'll use a balloon to tell the story today. If your child begs to do the balloon portion again, take the opportunity to reinforce the main point by repeating the words along with the illustration.

Mary packed her suitcase and hurried to visit her relative, Elizabeth. Up and down the hills of Judea Mary walked until she came to Elizabeth's door.

"Hello, Elizabeth. May God be gracious to you," Mary said.

Elizabeth was pregnant, and when she heard Mary's greeting, the baby inside her belly jumped. Elizabeth was filled with God's Spirit. Elizabeth said,

"Blessed are you among women, and blessed is the child you will bear!… As soon as the sound of your greeting reached my ears, the baby in my womb leaped for joy" (Luke 1:42, 44).

39

The baby boy inside Elizabeth's tummy was so glad he jumped for joy. The mother of Jesus was standing in his house. Immanuel was on his way!

Wherever God's Spirit is, there is joy (Galatians 5:22). If you have God's Spirit inside you, you can have joy too.

Sometimes that gladness is so big (*blow a deep breath into the balloon*), so great (*blow into the balloon again*), so powerful (*blow one last big breath into the balloon*), that you have to let it out (*release the balloon and watch it dart, dodge, and swirl around the room*).

When you have joy, you might leap or skip for joy. You might sing or laugh for joy. You might do cartwheels or climb a tree for joy.

How you show joy may be different than how someone else shows joy.

How do you like to show joy?

How does God show His joy through you?

:: **ADVENT ADVENTURE: CHRISTMAS TREE ORNAMENT** (OPT. 1) ::

SUPPLIES: Table covering (e.g., newspaper), pen, tree pattern (see page 132), cone-shaped coffee filter, water, scissors, colored markers, string or yarn

DIRECTIONS:

- Trace the tree pattern from page 132 onto a piece of paper.
- Fold the filter in half by bringing the two points together. Crease the fold.

- Line up the tree pattern with the fold you just made. Keep the tip of the tree at the tip of the cone filter.
- Cut out the pattern and unfold your tree.
- Cut a small hole at the top of the tree and thread a piece of string through the hole.
- Place the tree on the newspaper and use markers to place several large colored dots on the tree. Leave plenty of white space around each dot.
- Dip the tip of the pen into water and add a drop to the center of each dot.

What happens? The color bleeds from the center of the dot outward. When we have joy, it spreads to those around us. What are some ways you can spread joy?

:: Advent Adventure: Christmas Light (OPT. 2) ::

SUPPLIES: a squat wide-mouthed jar (like a salsa jar), light-colored wrapping paper, glue stick, tea light

DIRECTIONS:

- Cut a long strip of the wrapping paper that can be wrapped around the outside of the jar.
- Glue the paper to the outside of the jar.
- Place a tea light inside and light it.

When God's Spirit is inside us, like this candle is inside the jar, God's joy and light shine to everyone around.

I WONDER

Can I be sad about something and still have joy?

PRAYER TO SHARE

Dear God, thank You for Your joy that bubbles up inside me. When good things or bad things happen, I can have joy. You are always with me, always taking care of me. Amen.

CHRISTMAS COUNTDOWN

It's coming! It's coming!
Christmas is coming!
Only ___ more days until Christmas!

❄ DAY 8 ❄
BIGGER AND BETTER

Mary praises God. LUKE 1:46–55 NKJV

A magnifying glass makes everything look bigger—eyeballs, crickets, even M&Ms (don't you wish you could make an M&M bigger?). You magnified the _____ (*parents, fill in the blank with the first object you used*). You magnified the _____. You magnified the _____. You made them look bigger and better.

43

Mary magnified *God*. Not with a magnifying glass, of course, but with her words. She showed how big God is by what she said. Mary stood inside the door of Elizabeth's house, opened her mouth, and magnified God. Mary said...

My soul magnifies the Lord (Luke 1:46 NKJV).

Mary went on to say God is mighty; God does great things; God is perfect; God is strong (see Luke 1:49–51).

With every word, Mary showed that God is big. Unlike the things you magnified, God is always big. In fact, no matter how many good things you say about God, they will never be enough. He's that great.

What could *you* say to magnify God?

You don't magnify people the way you magnify God, but you can also use your words to make people feel bigger and better.

Your words can make people feel big, special, and important.

Your words can make people feel small, silly, and unimportant.

Your words can build people up.

Your words can tear people down.

Take turns with the magnifying glass. Look through it to the person on your right. Tell her what you like about him or her. For example, you could say "Mom, I like the blueberry pancakes you make," or "You have a pretty smile," or "You're a good hockey player." Hand the magnifying glass to the next person and let him take a turn.

When someone says something good about you, it makes you feel good inside. When other people hear you say good words to them, they feel good inside too. Choosing bigger and better words is better for everyone, including you.

JUST FOR FUN

The Song (or Canticle) of Mary found in Luke 1:46–55 sounds like a beautiful poem. Every word shows how big God is. Early manuscripts call it the Magnificat. Churches around the world today recite these verses during their services.

I WONDER

How big is God?

PRAYER TO SHARE

Dear God, I want to magnify You. I want to use my words
to show how great You are. You are very _____.
Help me remember to make others feel great too. Amen.

CHRISTMAS COUNTDOWN

It's coming! It's coming!
Christmas is coming!
Only ___ more days until Christmas!

GOOD WORDS OR NO WORDS

John is born, and Zechariah talks again. LUKE 1:57–80

:: **EXPLORE BEFORE** ::

Play this simple "What am I?" game with your child.
How many guesses will it take for you to discover what I am?
- I am one of the smallest parts of your body. *What am I?*
- I am made up of muscles that bend and twist. *What am I?*
- I am covered with little flavor bumps called taste buds. *What am I?*
- You use me to swallow and speak. *What am I?*
- I can taste bitter, sour, salty, and sweet. *What am I?*

Your tongue! When you sweep the tip off an ice cream cone or lick a lollipop down to the stick, when you swallow a mouthful of icy milk or make a silly face, you are using your tongue.

You can use your tongue for good things like telling a joke or singing a song. Or, you can use your tongue for not-so-good things.

Zechariah said a not-so-good thing. When the angel told Zechariah his wife, Elizabeth, would have a baby, Zechariah asked a question. Not an I-want-to-know question but an I-don't-believe-you question. So an angel hushed up his tongue. For months Zechariah pointed and waved, grunted and wrote. How he wished he could talk!

Take a few minutes and communicate without using your tongue.

After nine months, Elizabeth had the baby boy the angel had promised. Everyone was going to name the baby Zechariah.

> His mother spoke up and said, "No! He is to be called John." They said to her, "There is no one among your relatives who has that name." …He [Zechariah] asked for a writing tablet, and to everyone's astonishment he wrote, "His name is John." Immediately his mouth was opened and his tongue was loosed, and he began to speak, praising God (Luke 1:60–64).

Zechariah had learned his tongue lesson. The last words he spoke were not-so-good words. "I don't believe You, God," is really what he said. After John was born, his first words were super good words. He couldn't stop praising God.

How will you use *your* tongue?
What kind of words will *you* speak?

When thankful words pop out of your mouth, you make your dad or mom proud. When kind and true words tumble off your tongue, you make God happy. Good words make Him smile. Before you open your mouth, remember to speak good words. If you feel a bad or unkind word tickling the tip of your tongue, close your mouth quickly and speak no words instead.

:: ADVENT ADVENTURE: POPSICLE FUN (OPT. 1) ::

SUPPLIES: Eight 5-oz. paper cups with waxy coating (e.g., Dixie cups), 8 Popsicle sticks, 8"x8" pan, blender, 3 c. vanilla ice cream, ¾ c. orange juice, 8 strawberries

DIRECTIONS:

- Place the paper cups in the pan.
- Blend the ice cream, orange juice, and strawberries in a blender.
- Pour into paper cups and insert Popsicle sticks.
- Freeze several hours or overnight until solid.
- Peel off the paper and use your tongue to enjoy your Popsicles.

:: ADVENT ADVENTURE: SOMETHING'S MISSING SING-A-LONG (OPT. 2) ::

- Sing the chorus "O come let us adore Him." (Words are on page 93.)
- Sing it again, but when you get to the word "come," hum instead of singing the word.
- Sing it once more and hum for the words "come" and "adore."

How hard was it to remember to hum instead of sing? Trying to keep from saying a word takes concentration and practice. In the same way, teaching our tongues when and what to say takes practice too.

I WONDER

Why did God give me a tongue?

PRAYER TO SHARE

Dear God, let the words of my mouth and the thoughts of my heart make You smile. Amen. (Based on Psalm 19:14.)

CHRISTMAS COUNTDOWN

It's coming! It's coming!
Christmas is coming!
Only ___ more days until Christmas!

❄ DAY 10 ❄
A PARENT TO LOVE ME

*An angel tells Joseph that Mary's baby
is God's Son. MATTHEW 1:18–25*

Joseph wiped sweat off his forehead with the back of his hand. Sawdust clung to his hairy arms and face. He set aside his saw and closed his eyes. Mary had just told him she was expecting a baby. Joseph sighed. *I'm not the father of the baby. Who is?* he wondered. *I don't think I can marry her anymore.*

Joseph lay down on his mat that night and pulled his cloak around him. Questions and confusion zigzagged in his brain. As he fell asleep, he asked himself, *If I'm not the father of the baby, who is?* That night...

An angel of the Lord appeared to him in a dream and said, "Joseph, son of David, do not be afraid to take Mary home as your wife, because what is conceived in her is from the Holy Spirit. She will give birth to a son, and you are to give him the name Jesus, because he will save his people from their sins."... When Joseph woke up, he did what the angel of the Lord had commanded him and took Mary home as his wife (Matthew 1:20–24).

God was the Father of the baby stretching and growing inside Mary's tummy. But God lived in heaven and He wanted His Son to have a father on earth. A father who would pull Jesus up when He fell down. A father who'd show Him how to pound a nail, tell a joke, and scramble up a tree. A father Jesus could touch, see, smell, and hear.

Just like Jesus needed a dad, God knows you need someone to take care of you. A dad, a mom, or maybe a grandma who will hug you and pack your lunch for school. Someone who will teach you to tie your shoes and tuck you in at night. Most of all, though, God wants you to have someone who will show you what He's like.

Even if your child doesn't have both a mom and dad, asking these questions will give you a peek into what he's thinking:

- What do moms do? What do dads do?
- What's one thing you like about your (mom, dad)?
- When you grow up, what will you do with your kids?

:: ADVENT ADVENTURE: HOW WELL DO YOU KNOW MOM OR DAD? ::

Parents, if your child can read, have him ask you the questions that follow.
Otherwise, rephrase them into questions like the samples in parentheses.

1. When you were a kid, what chores did you do?
   What did you like to play?
   (What chores do you think I did when I was little?)
2. What did you want to be when you grew up?
   (What did you think I dreamed of being when I grew up?)
3. What's the best thing about being my mom (or dad)?
   (Why do you think I like being your mom/dad?)

I'm so thankful that God gave you to me. You are a gift from God.

Name Alert

__ __ __ __

I WONDER

What is God like? How is He like a parent?

PRAYER TO SHARE

Dear God, thank You for giving me a mom
(dad) I can touch and see and hear. Amen.

CHRISTMAS COUNTDOWN

It's coming! It's coming!
Christmas is coming!
Only ___ more days until Christmas!

❄ DAY 11 ❄
NO COMPLAINING

Joseph and Mary leave for Bethlehem. Luke 2:1–5

"Mary, we have to hurry," said Joseph. "I'm sorry. I know you're uncomfortable, but we have to get to Bethlehem." Caesar Augustus had ordered a census. Everyone in the whole Roman world had to be counted. Even though Mary was pregnant, she and…

> Joseph also went up from the town of Nazareth in Galilee to Judea, to Bethlehem the town of David, because he belonged to the house and line of David. He went there to register with Mary (Luke 2:4–5).

Joseph and Mary had no minivans or SUVs, no airplanes or trains. So Mary swayed *back-and-forth, back-and-forth* on top of a donkey while Joseph walked beside her. They traveled one day. Two days. Three days, then four.

Around them donkeys hee-hawed, soldiers marched, and people chatted. The smell of sweaty bodies filled the air, and gritty sand snuck into their mouths. Joseph's feet ached. Mary's back ached, and the unborn baby kicked and wiggled inside her.

As Joseph walked and Mary bumped along, they probably wondered, *Why do we have to go to Bethlehem now?*

Sometimes it's hard not to complain. Especially when...

You have to do something you don't want to do, like taking out the trash.

You got something you didn't want to get, like a cold.

You didn't get something you really did want, like a puppy for your birthday.

What are a few things that are hard for you to be thankful for?

Now, think about something good about each of your hard-to-be-thankful-for things. Maybe you don't like going to bed. But, you know that if you do, you'll have energy for the next day.

God watches over those who love Him and works out everything for their good. So look for the good in the things you don't like. If you can't find them, ask God to show you what they are. That's the kind of prayer that pleases Him.

Use your list of very good and not-so-very-good things to make the craft on the next page.

:: ADVENT ADVENTURE: WINDOWS ::

SUPPLIES: 1 piece construction paper, scissors, markers (or old magazines and glue stick)

DIRECTIONS:

- Fold the construction paper in half lengthwise.
- On one side, make two cuts up towards the fold, creating three equal flaps.
- Draw or cut out pictures of three of your not-so-favorite things. Glue them to the top of the flaps. For example, if you don't like going to bed, find a picture of a bed.
- Think of one good thing about each of your not-so-favorite things. Draw or cut out pictures that show those good things. For example, you might draw a picture of big muscles that represents the energy you'll get when you sleep.

Whenever you feel like complaining about _____ (*fill in the blank with one of your complaints*), take a peek under the flap and remember how what can seem like a bad thing can be a good thing.

I WONDER

How can I be thankful for something I don't like?

PRAYER TO SHARE

Dear God, please fill my mouth with thank-yous even when I don't feel like being thankful. Amen.

CHRISTMAS COUNTDOWN

It's coming! It's coming!
Christmas is coming!
Only ___ more days until Christmas!

HAPPY BIRTHDAY, JESUS!

Jesus is born. Luke 2:6–7

Knock-knock-knock. *Rap on a table or book.*
No answer.
Knock-knock-knock. *Rap again.*
No answer.
Knock-knock-knock. *Rap louder this time.*
"Can I help you?"
"My wife and I need a room, sir," said Joseph.
"Sorry, no rooms tonight."
"But we're going to have a baby. I mean, my wife is going to have a baby—soon."
"A baby! Hmm, well, we do have a stable where the animals stay."
A stable? thought Joseph. *A barn for camels and cows, donkeys and sheep?* That was no place for God's Son to be born. Yet that's exactly what happened.

While they were there, the time came for the baby to be born, and she [Mary] gave birth to her firstborn, a son. She wrapped him in cloths and placed him in a manger, because there was no room for them in the inn (Luke 2:6–7).

The baby whose name was…

Wonderful Counselor, Mighty God, Everlasting Father, Prince of Peace (Isaiah 9:6)

was born in a barn and slept in a feeding trough…
to the sound of bleating sheep, *baa baa;*
to the swaying of donkey tails, *swish swish;*
to the roaring of stubborn camels, *nuuuuur nuuuuur;*
to the munching of hungry oxen on golden grains of wheat, *crunch crunch.*

Jesus left His throne in heaven to sleep in a manger because of His great love for you and for me.

Name Alert: __ __ __ __ __ __ __ __ __ __

__ o __ __ __ __ __ __ __

__ __ __ __ __ __ G__ __

E __ __ __ __ __ __ __ __ __ __ F __ __ __ __ __

__ __ __ __ __ __ of P__ __ __ __

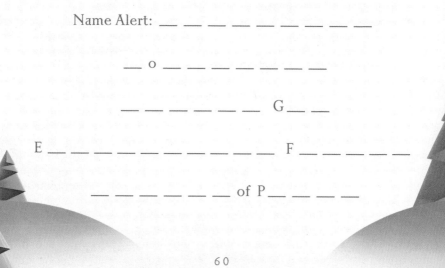

:: ADVENT ADVENTURE: CHRISTMAS PUPPET SHOW ::

Parents, even though it's not quite Christmas, have a pre-birthday celebration for Jesus and put on a puppet show. Have your child create these simple puppets, then use the script on page 63 to act out the part of the Christmas story he or she has learned so far.

SUPPLIES: 6 jumbo craft sticks, small googly eyes, miscellaneous decorations (e.g., pom-poms, cotton balls, fabric or flannel, markers, buttons)

DIRECTIONS:

- Glue two eyes onto each of the 6 craft sticks.
- Add miscellaneous decorations to personalize the following characters in your puppet show: angel, Zechariah, Elizabeth, Mary, Joseph, Baby Jesus.
- Invite a friend over and perform your puppet show or take turns performing it for each other.

I WONDER

What would it feel like to sleep in a stable?

PRAYER TO SHARE

Dear Jesus, thank You for leaving heaven
to come to earth. Amen.

CHRISTMAS COUNTDOWN

It's coming! It's coming!
Christmas is coming!
Only ___ more days until Christmas!

....
CHRISTMAS PUPPET SHOW
....

For younger children: *Designate an adult to read all the parts. Have the children duck behind a sofa or counter and manipulate the puppets as they're mentioned in the script.*

For older children: *Designate someone as narrator. Have the children practice their parts ahead of time or read their script from behind the counter or sofa while manipulating the puppets.*

ACT I

NARRATOR: Zechariah and Elizabeth were sad because they didn't have a baby. One day Zechariah walked into the temple and a bright angel appeared.

ANGEL: Guess what, Zechariah? You and Elizabeth are going to have a baby boy. The baby will grow up to be a prophet. Give him the name John.

ZECHARIAH: How do I know this is going to happen?

ANGEL: I am God's messenger. Because you didn't believe God's message, you won't be able to speak until everything comes true.

NARRATOR: The angel went back to heaven and Zechariah left the temple. Zechariah tried to talk but nothing came out. Soon Elizabeth found out she was having a baby. When the baby boy was born, her friends and family wanted to name the baby Zechariah.

ELIZABETH: No, the baby's name will be John.

NARRATOR: "But no one in your family has the name John," everyone said.

Zechariah asked for a piece of paper and he wrote, "The baby's name is John!" Suddenly Zechariah's mouth was opened and he could speak again. Everything that the angel had said had come true.

ACT II

NARRATOR: Six months after the angel went to Zechariah, God sent an angel to Mary. One day Mary was _____ (*use your imagination here*) when the angel showed up.

ANGEL: Mary, God is very happy with you. You're going to be the mother of His Son. His name will be Jesus.

MARY: How can I have a baby?

ANGEL: God's Spirit will come on you, and God's Son will grow inside you.

MARY: Okay.

ACT III

NARRATOR: Joseph was engaged to Mary. One night he fell asleep and had a dream. In the dream he saw an angel.

ANGEL: Joseph, the baby growing inside Mary is God's Son. You and Mary can get married.

NARRATOR: Joseph woke up, rubbed his eyes and smiled. Then he and Mary got married.

Soon Caesar said that everyone had to be counted. Joseph and Mary traveled all the way to Bethlehem, the place where they had to be counted. When they arrived, Joseph said...

JOSEPH: Excuse me, do you have a place where we could stay? *Knock, knock.* Do *you* have a place where we could stay? My wife is going to have a baby.

NARRATOR: There was no place for them in the inn, so they stayed in a stable. Jesus, the Son of God, was born, and Mary laid Him in a manger.

THE END

CELEBRATE THE PRINCE OF PEACE BY SINGING THIS SONG TOGETHER

AWAY IN A MANGER

Away in a manger,
No crib for His bed,
The little Lord Jesus
Laid down His sweet head
The stars in the bright sky
Look down where He lay
The little Lord Jesus
Asleep on the hay.

The cattle are lowing
The poor Baby wakes
But little Lord Jesus
No crying He makes
I love Thee, Lord Jesus,
Look down from the sky
And stay by my cradle
Till morning is nigh.

Verse 1 and 2, anon.; James R. Murray, Composer

SECTION 3

J O Y

"Joy means God's love
and it means you're joyful
and moving and having
a lot of fun."

ELIJAH, 6

HIGHLIGHTING JOY

Though we affirm that Christmas revolves around Jesus,
sometimes He's swallowed up in the very preparations
that claim to celebrate Him. This happens not because
we make preparations but because we neglect to spend
time in the presence of the One who gives us joy.

You have made known to me the paths of life;
you will fill me with joy in your presence.
ACTS 2:28

Happiness depends on happenings;
joy depends on Christ.
ANONYMOUS

ADVENT FAMILY ACTIVITY

Add a third candle, the JOY candle, to your evergreen boughs
and then tuck candy canes into the greenery. Each candy cane is
shaped like a J for Jesus and J for the joy He brings. Remember the
joy Mary, Joseph, the shepherds, and the Magi felt when they saw
the baby King.

JOY FOR PARENTS
DETOURS AND DESTINATIONS

Little children possess the remarkable ability to transform a few short steps into an endless journey. As a toddler, my son would squat in the middle of the sidewalk on the way from the house to the car.

"Ant," he'd say, pointing to a crumb-carrying creature.

"Yes, they're working hard," I'd respond. "Come, Davis."

He'd stand, walk three more steps, and squat again. "Rock," he'd say and scoop up a pebble.

I'd gently tug his arm. "Mommy has to go."

Davis would stand only to spot a butterfly. Finally I'd sweep him up and walk to the car.

I was on my way to complete an errand; Davis was on a journey to explore.

Conversations with little children don't progress any better. I sat cross-legged on the grass last spring and began unfolding the Easter story to two little neighborhood friends. Four-year-old Jude and six-year-old Delaney, however, seemed determined to sabotage my progress.

"I already know this story."

"Why didn't Judas like Jesus?"

"Why did the soldiers use nails?"

You're missing the point, I wanted to say. *It doesn't matter who didn't like Jesus or whether nails or arrows killed Him! Jesus is alive!*

I was on my way to the Resurrection; Jude and Delaney were on the way to—well, that was the problem. I'd never taken the time to find out.

Sometimes we're so focused on making a point that we bypass rich opportunities. We miss the joy of building relationships. When we encourage discussion, we say, "What you think and ask is important to me."

Lunging toward a destination also means we may miss the joy of a different destination. What if on that spring day, God was pointing me in a different direction than the one I'd set out to take? What if Jude and Delaney had glimpsed a hurting Jesus, someone rejected by a former friend?

When you sit down with your child and find yourself hijacked by seemingly off-the-point questions, listen to God's Spirit. Ask, "God, is this a path I should explore?" It could be that those distractions aren't detours at all—maybe they're new destinations.

A WHOLE LOT OF ANGELS

A group of angels praises God. LUKE 2:13

Parents, while making either one of the angel craft options, begin a conversation about angels using the text on the following page.

:: TERRA COTTA ANGEL (OPT. 1) ::

SUPPLIES: Table covering (e.g., newspaper), 4" terra cotta pot, 3" or 4" Styrofoam ball, 1 bottle of gold acrylic craft paint, paintbrush, white card stock or craft foam (roughly 9"x12"), glitter glue, all-purpose glue, angel wing pattern (see page 133)

DIRECTIONS:
- Turn the terra cotta pot upside down onto the newspaper.
- Paint the pot with gold paint and allow to dry.
- Use glitter glue to create eyes and a mouth on the Styrofoam "head."
- From the pattern on page 133, trace two angel wings onto the card stock and cut out the wings.
- Line the edges of the wings with glitter glue and let dry.

- Tape or glue the wings to the back of the pot.
- Place a generous amount of glue around the bottom (now the top) of the pot, glue the head on, and allow the glue to dry.

:: PAPER CHAIN ANGELS (OPT. 2) ::

SUPPLIES: one 8½"x11" sheet of paper, scissors, pen or pencil, angel pattern (see page 134)

DIRECTIONS:
- Fold the paper in half lengthwise.
- Tear along the fold line, making two strips of paper.
- Fold each strip in half once and then again.
- Draw the angel design from page 134 on the folded paper.
- Cut out around the angel outline then unfold your angel paper chain.

Have you ever noticed the Christmas story has a whole lot of angels? An angel surprised Zechariah in the temple. An angel dropped by to see Mary, then Joseph. When Jesus was born, an angel appeared to the shepherds and "there appeared with the angel a multitude of the heavenly host praising God" (Luke 2:13 NASB).

What are angels anyway?

Angels are messengers of God. More than 100 million angels serve God and report for duty (Revelation 5:11). God puts angels in charge of children (Matthew 18:10), churches (Revelation 1:20), and even whole nations like Israel (Daniel 12:1).

God calls angels "mighty ones" (Psalm 103:20). They can hold back the wind (Revelation 7:1) or clamp down the jaws of a lion (Daniel 6:22). One powerful angel rolled away the stone in front of Jesus' tomb (Matthew 28:2).

Angels have names like we do. We only know two angel names. The angel Michael was in charge of the people of Israel (Daniel 12:1). Gabriel was the name of the angel who visited Zechariah and Mary (Luke 1:19, 26).

What do angels look like?

Angels are spirits (Hebrews 1:14). They don't have bodies—no elbows, eyeballs, or knuckles—so we usually can't see them. When they do appear, angels shine with a bright light and wear white robes, sometimes with a golden sash (Revelation 18:1; John 20:12; Revelation 15:6).

Other times, angels can look like regular people. The Bible says to invite guests into your home, and (with your parents' permission) even guests you don't know. Why? You may be entertaining an angel in disguise (Hebrews 13:2).

What do angels do?

Angels can do just about everything! They deliver messages and burst open jail doors (Acts 5:19). They carry people to heaven when they die (Luke 16:22). And angels love to party! When someone turns away from sin, the angels celebrate (Luke 15:10).

No matter what an angel looks like or what an angel does, an angel serves one person—the Lord God (Psalm 103:20). Angels are *God's* servants, mighty ones that do *His* bidding, exactly what He says. Before this Christmas story is over, you'll see God put a whole lot more angels to work.

I WONDER

Why do angels shine? (See Luke 2:9.)

PRAYER TO SHARE

Dear God, thank You for the mighty angels
that You send to care for me. Amen.

CHRISTMAS COUNTDOWN

It's coming! It's coming!
Christmas is coming!
Only ___ more days until Christmas!

❄ DAY 14 ❄
SCARED SHEPHERDS

Angels appear to the shepherds. LUKE 2:8–14

What would your life be like if you were a shepherd?

You'd fill your days herding sheep and searching for clumps of juicy grass. You'd water the sheep and guard them from bears or wolves. You'd care for little lambs and stop sometimes to scratch their woolly heads and ears.

What if one day had been a really looong day. One sheep had tangled his legs in a bush. A ewe had wandered off with her lamb. The sun had waved good-bye, and the stars said hello. You smelled like sheep manure; your stomach was complaining. Your eyelids sagged and you just wanted to eat a hot bowl of soup, when all of a sudden—an angel showed up!

That's what happened to the shepherds at Bethlehem. They were out on a starlit night, minding their own business, when—BAM!— a real live angel appeared.

> An angel of the Lord appeared to them, and the glory of the Lord shone around them, and they were terrified (Luke 2:9).

The shepherds were terrified,
>scared,
>frightened,
>filled up with fear.
What was going on?

>*But the angel said to them, "Do not be afraid. I bring you good news of great joy that will be for all the people. Today in the town of David a Savior has been born to you; he is Christ the Lord. This will be a sign to you: You will find a baby wrapped in cloths and lying in a manger"* (Luke 2:10–12).

When the shepherds heard God's good news, their fear turned into joy.

Have you ever been terrified,
>scared,
>frightened,
>filled up with fear?

(If your child answered yes, ask him or her to tell you about one of those times.) Just like God had good news for the shepherds, God has good news for you: "Do not be afraid, for I am with you" (Isaiah 43:5). God wants to dump out your fear and fill you up with

joy. Not just itty-bitty joy but Big Joy, GREAT JOY! Wherever God goes, He brings joy along with Him. So if He's with you, His joy comes along too, and fear just has to—go!

:: ADVENT ADVENTURE: JOY IN A JAR ::

SUPPLIES: Small jar, large jar, dish soap, food coloring
DIRECTIONS:
- Place a little water and some dish soap in the small jar.
- Shake the jar until it's full of bubbles.
- Fill the large jar with water and add food coloring.
- Slowly pour the colored water into the jar of bubbles.

What happened to the bubbles? When you poured in the colorful water, the bubbles tumbled out the top. We're like the jar, and the bubbles are like fear. When we pray and ask God to be with us, He pours His joy inside us and our fear comes tumbling out.

Name Alert

___ ___ ___ ___ ___ ___

___ ___ ___ ___ ___ ___ the ___ ___ ___ ___

I WONDER

If joy were a color, what color would it be?

PRAYER TO SHARE

Dear God, I don't want to be afraid of _____
(*fill in the blank*) anymore. Please pour Your joy
inside me and send my fear away. Amen.

CHRISTMAS COUNTDOWN

It's coming! It's coming!
Christmas is coming!
Only ___ more days until Christmas!

❄ DAY 15 ❄

GOOD NEWS AND BEAUTIFUL FEET

The shepherds spread the good news
of Jesus' birth. LUKE 2:15–18

:: EXPLORE BEFORE ::

Check out The Foot Book *by Dr. Seuss from your local library*
and read it together.
Have everyone strip off their socks and describe their feet.
Are they bony feet, soft feet, maybe even dirty feet?

Have you ever heard of a shepherd who has beautiful feet? All day long shepherds hike through mud and dust and scrubby brush, finding the best places for their sheep to graze. Shepherds might have stinky feet, dry feet, maybe even sore feet, but beautiful feet? Here's the story of a few shepherds who had beautiful feet.

One night hundreds of shining angels spread across the sky. "A Savior has been born in Bethlehem," they said to the shepherds.

"You'll find the baby wrapped in cloth, lying in a manger." Then the angels vanished as quickly as they came. Light disappeared; blackness swallowed up the sky. Angel voices faded; quietness moved in. *Hush.*

"Did you see what I saw?" asked one shepherd, scratching his head.

"Did you hear what I heard?" asked another shepherd, stroking his chin.

> "Let's go to Bethlehem and see this thing that has happened, which the Lord has told us about." So they hurried off and found Mary and Joseph, and the baby, who was lying in the manger (Luke 2:15–16).

Everything the angels had said was true!

> When they had seen him [the baby], they spread the word concerning what had been told them about this child (Luke 2:17).

The shepherds' feet carried them home. They hurried to the sheepfold. They shuffled through the marketplace. Everywhere their feet carried them the shepherds told family and friends about the newborn baby. They spread good news by using their feet.

Those who tell the good news about God have beautiful feet (Isaiah 52:7). If you tell the good news that Jesus was born, your feet become beautiful too. As you skip to your cousin's house, dash to the play-ground, or walk down the halls at school, you can tell aunts and uncles, grandmas and grandpas, neighbors and friends about Jesus. "Guess what?" you might say. "God loved us so much He sent Jesus to be born."

When you do that, God just might look at your feet and say, "Wow, you've got some beautiful feet."

Where can your feet take you to tell someone about Jesus?

:: ADVENT ADVENTURE: GOOD FEET GREETING CARD ::

SUPPLIES: 1 piece construction paper, washable paint, paintbrush, pencil—and a little imagination

DIRECTIONS:

CREATE A "FOOT"

- Fold the construction paper in half to make a card.
- Make a fist and brush paint onto the pinky end of your fist.
- Press down onto the front of the card to create a "footprint."
- Next, brush paint onto the tip of one of your fingers.
- Press down around the top of the footprint to create "toes."

ADD THE POEM

- Choose four sets of opposite words to describe feet (e.g., cold/hot; green/red).

- Insert your words into the poem below, and copy the poem on the inside of your card. Or, ask your mom or dad to write it for you.
- Give the card to a friend or to someone who doesn't know Jesus.

_____ feet, _____ feet
_____ feet, _____ feet

Feet, sweet feet.
How many, many,
feet you meet.

_____ feet, _____ feet
_____ feet, _____ feet

Good news feet.
The very, very, very
best feet to meet.

My feet and I bring you the good news of Jesus this Christmas.

[Sign your name]

How beautiful on the mountains are the feet
of those who bring good news.
ISAIAH 52:7.

I WONDER

What's the farthest place someone's feet could take them?

PRAYER TO SHARE

Dear God, make my feet beautiful. Show me where I
can go and who I can tell about Jesus' birth. Amen.

CHRISTMAS COUNTDOWN

It's coming! It's coming!
Christmas is coming!
Only ___ more days until Christmas!

CELEBRATE WHAT FEET CAN DO BY SINGING THIS SONG TOGETHER

GO TELL IT ON THE MOUNTAIN

CHORUS:
Go, tell it on the mountain,
Over the hills and everywhere
Go, tell it on the mountain,
That Jesus Christ is born.

While shepherds kept their watching
O'er silent flocks by night
Behold, throughout the heavens
There shone a holy light.

CHORUS

The shepherds feared and trembled,
When lo! above the earth,
Rang out the angel chorus
That hailed the Savior's birth.

CHORUS

Down in a lowly manger
The humble Christ was born
And God sent us salvation
That blessed Christmas morn.

John W. Work, Jr.

WHAT'S IN A NAME?

Simeon and Anna meet Jesus in the temple. LUKE 2:22–38

When Jesus was six weeks old, Joseph and Mary took a cooing, drooling, smiley Jesus to the temple. There they dedicated Him to God.

> As it is written in the Law of the Lord, "Every firstborn male is to be consecrated to the Lord" (Luke 2:23).

While at the temple, they met Simeon. Simeon means "hearing," and that morning Simeon *heard* God.

"Simeon, go to the temple," God said.

Simeon finished his breakfast and hurried to the temple. There, he *heard* God again.

"Simeon, see that baby over there? That is the Christ."

Simeon went over to Joseph and Mary and asked, "Can I please pick him up?" He scooped baby Jesus up in his arms, and he heard God again. Then Simeon gave Mary God's message, the words God had said.

Just then the prophetess Anna walked up. Anna means "grace" or "favor." God showed favor to Anna—she got to meet God's Son! She told everyone who'd listen, "The Christ child is born!"

Just like "Simeon" has a meaning and "Anna" has a meaning, your name has a meaning too.

What do you think your name means?

Go to The Family Book of Advent link under www.faithfamilystyle.com to learn the meaning of your name.

Why did your parents choose your name? Were you named after a grandparent or a close friend?

What does your name say about the kind of person you are?

> PARENT TIP: *Not every name has a spiritual meaning. If that's the case for your child, focus on a middle name. Or, explore other positive aspects of your child's name. Chase, for example, means "hunter," "to follow or look for." Chase might not be a boy who hunts rabbits and squirrels, but he could become a person who's inquisitive and "hunts or looks for" interesting facts.*

If you belong to Jesus, you're part of God's family. You are _____ (*fill in the blank with your name*), a son or daughter in God's family.

Whatever your name is, honor it. A good name is better than sweet perfume (Ecclesiastes 7:1). Give everyone a reason to think good things about you and your name. Live it out in a way that makes God smile.

:: Advent Adventure: Name Collage ::

SUPPLIES: All-purpose glue, poster board, marker, photos, small objects
DIRECTIONS:
- To make your collage, collect different objects and pictures that represent...
    - the meaning of your name,
    - the people for whom you were named,
    - the story of how you were born.
  If your name is Samuel, "asked of God," you could find a picture of praying hands. If you were named after a grandma who likes to sew, you could find a button for your collage.
- At the top of the poster board write, "What's in My Name?"
- Glue items and pictures to the poster board.

I WONDER

How many names are there in the world?
How does God keep them straight?

PRAYER TO SHARE

Dear God, thank You for making me *me* and for
giving me my name. Help me to honor my name.
Most of all, help me to honor Yours. Amen.

CHRISTMAS COUNTDOWN

It's coming! It's coming!
Christmas is coming!
Only ___ more days until Christmas!

❄ DAY 17 ❄
FOLLOW THE STAR

The Magi follow the star. MATTHEW 2:1–2

:: **EXPLORE BEFORE** ::

SUPPLIES: A dark room, flashlight, Bible

DIRECTIONS:

Hide a few items around the house to prepare your child for family time (e.g., a stuffed animal, a sleeping bag).

Next, turn off the lights, stand in one spot, and lead your child to the various items by shining a flashlight on the ceiling, stopping over the sleeping bag, etc. You might lead him to a pillow, a bowl of popcorn, and finally to a Bible.

Turn to Matthew 2:1–2 and read...

After Jesus was born in Bethlehem in Judea, during the time of King Herod, Magi [wise men] from the east came to Jerusalem and asked, "Where is the one who has been born king of the Jews? We saw his star in the east and have come to worship him."

Stars were sprinkled across the black sky the night Jesus was born. But a special star sparkled over Bethlehem, a star of a king.

The Magi saw the star. The Magi followed the star. The Magi traveled to worship Jesus.

Over rivers, across deserts, through valleys the wise men traveled. Finally they stepped onto the crowded streets of Jerusalem.

"Where is the King of the Jews?" they asked.

"King of the Jews? Herod the Great is king," someone said.

"We're looking for a different king," the wise men answered. "The King whose star rose high in the sky."

Everyone kept insisting that Herod was king. But the Magi knew the Bethlehem star pointed to Jesus.

The Bethlehem star isn't the only star that points to Jesus. Each fiery star praises God. The planets, the moon, and the entire galaxy praise God. God created them by the breath of His mouth (Psalm 33:6).

Can you think of something that's above the earth? (*A rainbow?*)

Can you think of something that lives on the earth? (*A hippopotamus?*)

How about something that lives under the earth? (*A gopher?*)

Everything in the heavens, on the earth, and under the earth praises the Lord.

The heavens shout (Psalm 19:1). *Have your child shout.*

The earth trembles (Psalm 97:4). *Have your child shake.*

The sea roars (Psalm 98:7). *Have your child roar.*

The mountains sing (Psalm 98:8). *Fa-la-la-la-la.*

The rivers clap (Psalm 98:8). *Clap.*

And they're all doing one thing—praising God! *Raise hands up.*

Whenever you spy purple, orange, and pink clouds streaked across the sky, when icy rain stings your face, when you breathe in the sweetness of a rose or laugh at a pig's *oink-oink*, when you crunch into an apple and juice drips down your chin, remember that all creation points to the God who made them. Just like the Bethlehem star pointed to Jesus.

Name Alert

___ ___ ___ ___ of the ___ ___ ___ ___

What's one thing in creation that
makes me want to praise Jesus?

PRAYER TO SHARE

Dear God, when I look at the heavens, the moon and
the stars You put in place, I think it's awesome that
You care about me. Amen. (Based on Psalm 8:3–4.)

CHRISTMAS COUNTDOWN

It's coming! It's coming!
Christmas is coming!
Only ___ more days until Christmas!

IMAGINE FOLLOWING THE STAR WITH THE MAGI AS YOU SING THIS SONG TOGETHER

O COME, ALL YE FAITHFUL

O come, all ye faithful
Joyful and triumphant,
Come ye, O come ye to Bethlehem;
Come and behold Him,
Born the King of Angels;

CHORUS:
O come, let us adore Him,
O come, let us adore Him,
O come, let us adore Him,
Christ the Lord.

Sing, choirs of angels,
Sing in exultation,
Sing all ye bright hosts of heav'n above;
Glory to God, all glory in the highest;

CHORUS

Frederick Oakeley, Translator. From John F. Wade's *Cantus Diversi*

❄ DAY 18 ❄
JUST ONE KING

King Herod is jealous of Jesus.
MATTHEW 2:3–8

:: EXPLORE BEFORE ::

DIRECTIONS:
• *Choose one person to be the leader.*
• *Follow the leader as she walks, jumps, crawls through the house, out to the garage, etc.*
Parents, when you're done, ask,
"How would you play this game if we had two leaders instead of one? Could you follow both? Why or why not? Today we're going to read about a man who knew there could just be one leader, one king."

King Herod had a crown and a throne, servants and soldiers. He built palaces, temples, theaters, and forts. He attacked lands, captured cities, and ruled a country. King Herod was a powerful king.

Then the Magi started asking questions about a *new* King. King Herod wasn't very happy.

94

He was disturbed, and all Jerusalem with him. When he had called together all the people's chief priests and teachers of the law, he asked them where the Christ was to be born. "In Bethlehem in Judea," they replied (Matthew 2:3–5).

"When you find the baby in Bethlehem," Herod said to the Magi, "come back and let me know."

Someday, Herod knew, a new king, the Christ, would come. If a new king came, King Herod would lose his crown and his country, his throne and his army. He'd lose his palaces, forts, and all of his cities. Worst of all, though, King Herod would lose his power. Everyone would listen to the new king; no one would listen to him.

King Herod knew there could be just one king. He wanted to be that king.

Every day you decide who will be your king (or your leader). If Mom says, "Time to come in for supper," and your friend says, "You can play longer," you have to choose whom to follow. If God says, "Don't lie," and your friend says, "Go ahead and lie," you have to choose whom to follow. Who will be your king? Who will be your leader?

:: ADVENT ADVENTURE: THE BEST KING ::

SUPPLIES: Handful of sand (or salt or sugar)
DIRECTIONS:

Say the following to your child:

Stand up then sit down. *Have your child stand up then sit down.*

Look behind you, now in front of you. *Continue with the actions.*

Think about your favorite ice cream but don't say what it is.

Now try to count these tiny grains of sand. *Place a pinch of sand in his palm.*

Jesus is God, King over everything.

He knows when you sit and knows when you stand.

He goes behind you, before you, and His hand rests on you.

He knows what you're thinking when no one else does.

If you could count His thoughts toward you they would be more than the grains of sand at the seashore. (Based on Psalm 139.)

Jesus isn't just the only King; He's the best King.

Name Alert

___ ___ ___ i ___ ___

I WONDER

What would happen if there were two
presidents instead of one?

PRAYER TO SHARE

Dear Jesus, I want You to be the King of my life
and the Leader of my family. I want to follow
You. You're the best King of all. Amen.

CHRISTMAS COUNTDOWN

It's coming! It's coming!
Christmas is coming!
Only ___ more days until Christmas!

SECTION 4

LOVE

"Love is when you
kiss and hug people.
I know somebody loves
me when they
take care of me."

ADRIAH, 5

HIGHLIGHTING LOVE

The saddest part of sin is that it keeps us from having a relationship
with the One who loves us more than the whole world. How that
makes His heart ache! So God, who is love, made plans to bring
us back where we belong—in close relationship with Him.

For God so loved the world that he gave his
one and only Son, that whoever believes in him
shall not perish but have eternal life.
JOHN 3:16

God loves each of us as if there were only one of us.
AUGUSTINE

ADVENT FAMILY ACTIVITY

Add a fourth candle, the LOVE candle, to the evergreen boughs and
place pinecones all around. Pinecones represent life, the seeds deep
inside them waiting to burst open. Because God loved us so much, He
sent His Son, the Way, the Truth, and the Life, to give *us* everlasting
life. Nothing can separate us from that love.

LOVE FOR PARENTS
GOD'S LOVE THROUGHOUT GENERATIONS

From the time our son was a toddler, my husband and I read him Bible stories. We breezed through Jonah and plodded through Exodus and explored the heroes of faith. What more could we do though, I wondered, to encourage him to grasp God's truth as his own?

One day, my husband and I invited our friend Pastor Vargas and his wife over for lunch, and they began telling stories. Since they can turn an ordinary account into front-seat entertainment, I settled in to listen.

While in college, Vargas was painting a wall on a scaffolding eighteen feet high. He fell and shattered his arm in several places. Because of the swelling, doctors scheduled surgery for the following day.

In the pre-op room the next morning, nurses unwrapped the bandages around his arm and found no evidence of broken bones! X-rays confirmed his arm was completely healed.

I sat entranced, my lunch forgotten. Reading about a miracle was one thing; sitting at the table with one was another. That was when I realized what was missing in my own family. I needed to pair Bible stories with stories of my own. I had to show my son that the God of then was also the God of now.

Psalm 145:4 says, "One generation will commend your works to another; they will tell of your mighty acts." We need to tell our children *our* stories, testimonies of God's love for us. Face it, we're far more impressed when we know the person involved in the stories we hear.

You might be saying...

"But I don't have any testimonies." Ask God to retrieve memories of His love for you. How He answered a prayer for a job. How He painted your childhood sunsets with colors you'll never forget.

"I can't think of anything dramatic." The God of mountains is the God of minnows. A minnow doesn't snatch your breath away like Mt. Everest does, but examine it closely and you can't help but come away fascinated. In it, you'll discover something perhaps not as grand but no less miraculous.

"How do I tell my kids?" You'll find little children forgivable. They're the perfect ones on whom to practice. If they don't understand, they're never shy about asking a question. If your child is heading into the teen years, stories open the door to otherwise closed ears. If you were a teenager, what would you rather hear: "You need to forgive that person" or "I know how you feel. Once a friend of mine hurt my feelings. Let me tell you about..."?

Share your stories with your kids. Not when-I-was-your-age stories but the God-loved-me stories of your life. As you testify of God's love, you'll see your own faith grow as well as theirs.

❄ DAY 19 ❄
GIFTS FOR A KING

The Magi give gifts to Jesus. MATTHEW 2:9–11

B ethlehem! So that's where the newborn King is," said the Magi. They waved good-bye to King Herod, climbed on their camels, and bumped along the five-mile road to Bethlehem.

Finally we get to meet the new King, they thought. *Can't these camels move any faster?*

Bump. Bump-bump. Bumpity-bump-bump-bump.

The Magi followed the star until it stood over Jesus' house.

> When they saw the star, they rejoiced with exceedingly great joy. And when they had come into the house, they saw the young Child with Mary His mother, and fell down and worshiped Him. And when they had opened their treasures, they presented gifts to Him: gold, frankincense, and myrrh (Matthew 2:10–11 NKJV).

The wise men were…
    so filled with awe,
        so bubbling with joy,
            so bursting with love,

that they worshiped Jesus and gave Him the gifts of a king—gold, frankincense, and myrrh.

When you love Jesus, you want to worship Him (tell Him how much you love Him). One way to worship Him is to give Him gifts.

What could you give to Jesus? Any ideas?

Here are a few.

What do you say at the table when someone passes the mashed potatoes? *Thank you!* He likes it when you give Him thanks. (See Psalm 107:1.)

If your dad were across the ball field from you, what would you do so he could hear you? *Shout.* He likes when you give Him shouts of joy. (See Psalm 98:4.)

What do people sometimes do when they're listening to music? *Sing.* He likes when you sing to Him. (See Ephesians 5:19.)

Of all the gifts you can give to Jesus, though, what He really wants is just YOU!

:: ADVENT ADVENTURE: WALL HANGING ::

SUPPLIES: 2 feet of wide ribbon, 1 (8½"x11") piece of card stock, all-purpose glue, markers , old magazines, scissors

DIRECTIONS:

- Fold the card stock in half once and then a second time.
- Cut along the folds to make four separate panels.
- At the top of each panel write one of these words:
  I...Worship...the...Lord!
- Find pictures that illustrate singing, praising, thanking, and shouting and cut them out. For thanking, you could find a picture of food you're thankful for. For shouting, you could find a picture of someone with their mouth open wide. Or, simply draw pictures.
- Glue the pictures onto the card stock panels, directly underneath the words. Then glue the panels onto a long ribbon and hang the decoration on the wall.

Gold is beautiful. Nothing can take away its glitter and shine. Gold is also very valuable.

Frankincense comes from a tree. People burned it in offerings or used it in perfume.

Myrrh means bitter so you wouldn't want to eat it. But it smells like perfume and was used to make the anointing oil of kings.

I WONDER

I wonder what present Jesus liked most: gold, frankincense, or myrrh? What present did His mom like best?

PRAYER TO SHARE

Dear Jesus, I worship You. I give You my
life and all that I am. Amen.

CHRISTMAS COUNTDOWN

It's coming! It's coming!
Christmas is coming!
Only ___ more days until Christmas!

❄ DAY 20 ❄
LICKETY-SPLIT

Joseph, Mary, and Jesus escape to Egypt. MATTHEW 2:12–14

The Magi waved good-bye to Joseph, Mary, and Jesus and climbed onto their camels. It was time to go back to King Herod and tell him they'd found Jesus. But…

Having been warned in a dream not to go back to Herod, they returned to their country by another route. When they had gone, an angel of the Lord appeared to Joseph in a dream. "Get up," he said, "take the child and his mother and escape to Egypt. Stay there until I tell you, for Herod is going to search for the child to kill him." So he [Joseph] got up, took the child and his mother during the night and left for Egypt" (Matthew 2:12–14).

Can you imagine Joseph saying to the angel…
- "What? I have to go all the way to Egypt?"
- "Are you sure?"
- "I'd better pray about this first."
- "I need a good night's rest (*yawn*). We'll leave in the morning."

Joseph didn't wait for morning; he fled when stars speckled the sky.

"Let's go, let's go, let's go!"

Joseph kicked off the covers and jumped up off his mat. "Wake up, Mary. Hurry!" Joseph grabbed food and filled a goatskin with water. He wrapped up the gifts of gold, frankincense, and myrrh. He scooped up a sleeping Jesus and stepped out the door with Mary. Lickety-split, just like that, the family was on their way to Egypt.

God longs for us to be quick to listen and obey like Joseph. When your mom says, "Get ready for bed," or "Please empty the dishwasher," what do you say?
- "But, Mom! Do I have to?"
- "You mean right now?"
- "In a minute, as soon as I finish…"
- "Sure."

When you're not *quick* to obey, you're *slow* to obey. Being slow to obey means disobeying a little longer. That makes your dad or mom sad inside. But if you answered "sure," you put a big smile on their faces. Because they love you, what they tell you to do comes out of a big heart bursting with love. The things God tells you to do come from a heart full of love too, so be quick to obey.

:: ADVENT ADVENTURE: WORD PUZZLE ::

Use the clues in parentheses to fill in the blanks with the correct letters.

_____ (what _____ you thinking?)

_____ (me, myself, and _____)

_____ (*say* the first syllable of the newborn King's name)

_____ (some children are in a 4-___ club)

_____ (tickle Tom's toes today)

_____ (first letter of the alphabet)

_____ (two u's)

_____ (one of three letters that rhymes with "day")

_____ (_____ did the chicken cross the road?)

Do what your parents say __ __ __ __ __   __ __ __ __

How is obeying a good thing for me?

PRAYER TO SHARE

Dear God, "I will hurry, without delay, to obey
Your commands." Please remind me to be quick
to obey. Amen. (Based on Psalm 119:60 NLT).

CHRISTMAS COUNTDOWN

It's coming! It's coming!
Christmas is coming!
Only ___ more days until Christmas!

SAFE AND SOUND

Herod sends his soldiers to Bethlehem. MATTHEW 2:16–18

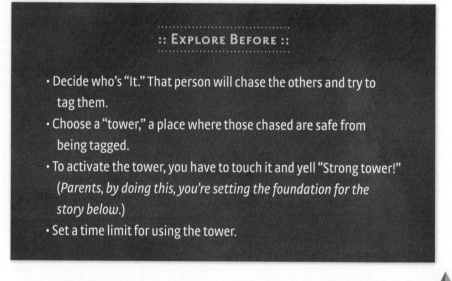

:::::::::::::::::::::::::::::::::::
:: EXPLORE BEFORE ::
:::::::::::::::::::::::::::::::::::

- Decide who's "It." That person will chase the others and try to tag them.
- Choose a "tower," a place where those chased are safe from being tagged.
- To activate the tower, you have to touch it and yell "Strong tower!" (*Parents, by doing this, you're setting the foundation for the story below.*)
- Set a time limit for using the tower.

The Magi tricked me!" King Herod shouted. "They didn't listen to what I said. I told them 'As soon as you find the baby, report to me so I can worship him.' *That's* what I said."

When Herod realized that he had been outwitted by the Magi, he was furious (Matthew 2:16).

With a shout King Herod ordered soldiers to Bethlehem. "The baby 'King' will not escape!" he said.

But Jesus did escape.

Mary, Joseph, and Jesus were already safe.

Safe from King Herod's anger.

Safe from the soldiers' swords.

Far away in Egypt.

Like a strong tower protects those inside, God protects those He loves. (See Proverbs 18:10.) He keeps them safe. Just like God kept Joseph, Mary, and Jesus safe, He keeps you safe.

When does God protect you? *Always!*

Whether you're eating Cheerios, studying math, or throwing a snowball, God is protecting you. When you're _____ (*parents, fill in the blank with something your child typically does*), God is protecting you.

Where does God protect you? *Everywhere!*

Whether you're on the school bus, in the living room, or tucked in bed, God is protecting you. When you're _____ (*again, fill in the blank with places your child typically goes*), God is protecting you.

Why does God protect you? *Because He loves you.*

He protects you always and everywhere because He loves you. He is your strong tower.

:: ADVENT ADVENTURE: BUILD A TOWER ::

Create a four-sided tower with Legos or blocks, or use the directions below to make a more elaborate sugar cube tower.

SUPPLIES: Box of sugar cubes (next to the regular sugar in the grocery store), all-purpose glue, ruler, paper, pencil, paper plate

DIRECTIONS:

- Decide how large the square base of your tower will be. (Suggested size: 3"—the larger the base, the longer the attention span required)
- Draw your square onto a piece of paper.
- Cut out the square and place it on a paper plate.
- Glue the sugar cubes together, using the square as a guide. Place a dot of glue on the side of the first sugar cube and place it on the square. Do the same with the next sugar cube. Be generous with the glue. Use your imagination and create parapets, windows, etc.

Proverbs 18:10 says "The name of the LORD is a strong tower; the righteous run to it and are safe." Remember that God is like your strong tower. Just call for help, and He will keep you safe.

I WONDER

How strong is God?

PRAYER TO SHARE

Dear God, when I go to bed, I can lie down in peace and get good sleep. You are the One who keeps me safe. Amen. (Based on Psalm 4:8.)

CHRISTMAS COUNTDOWN

It's coming! It's coming!
Christmas is coming!
Only ___ more days until Christmas!

❄ DAY 22 ❄
HOME AGAIN, HOME AGAIN

Jesus and His family go home
to Nazareth. MATTHEW 2:19–23

oseph, do you ever think about home?" Mary asked.

Joseph and Mary had made many new friends in Egypt. Still, they remembered the family and friends they'd left behind. Mary remembered walking to Nazareth's only well and filling up her jar with water. She remembered laughing with her neighbors and grinding flour with her friends. Joseph remembered working in his father's woodshop and eating handfuls of salty olives. Wouldn't it be great to go home?

One night...

> an angel of the Lord appeared in a dream to Joseph in Egypt and said, "Get up, take the child and his mother and go to the land of Israel, for those who were trying to take the child's life are dead" (Matthew 2:19–21).

Home! Joseph threw off the covers and jumped off his mat. "Guess what, Mary? We get to go home!" Joseph filled a goatskin with water. Mary wrapped up cheese and bread. In the cool of

morning, Joseph woke up a sleepy Jesus and stepped out the door. Their family was going back to Nazareth—home!

Slap, slap, slap went three pairs of sandals against the stone road.

Slap, slap, slap went three pairs of sandals walking (skipping!) home.

With every step, they remembered how God had been faithful to protect and take care of them.

When the angel announced, "Mary, you're going to have a baby!" God was faithful.

When they trekked the long road to Bethlehem, God was faithful.

When there was no room in the inn, God was _____ (*have your child fill in the blank*).

When smelly shepherds crowded around the manger, God was

_____ .

When Magi arrived with treasure chests, God was _____ .

When the family escaped to Egypt, God was _____ .

God was still faithful now. He was taking them home!

Sometimes you have to take time to remember what God has done for you, so you don't forget His kindness. Think of a time when God has taken care of you. Then, thank God for being faithful. He's Someone you can believe and trust.

:: Advent Adventure: Memory Making ::

Create a new family tradition (or at least try it on for size). Make the hot chocolate recipe below together (or warm up apple cider or just make instant cocoa). Then gather around the Christmas tree or light several candles. Take a couple minutes to remember happy times, funny times, maybe even sad times.

I remember when...

My favorite Christmas memory was when....

SUPPLIES: 4 c. milk, ½ c. chocolate chips, 1 c. marshmallow creme (not marshmallow topping), 1 tsp. vanilla, sprinkles or crushed candy canes, malted milk balls (optional)

DIRECTIONS:

Heat the milk in a saucepan until it barely starts to bubble around the edges. Remove from heat. Add chocolate and marshmallow creme and whisk together. Add the vanilla. Pour into mugs and top with an additional spoonful of marshmallow creme. Sprinkle with crushed candy canes or sprinkles, and top with a malted milk ball. Serves 4.

I WONDER

Where is God when I'm happy?
Where is God when I'm sad?

PRAYER TO SHARE

Dear God, thank You for taking care of me in happy times. Thank You for taking care of me in sad times. You are always faithful. Amen.

CHRISTMAS COUNTDOWN

It's coming! It's coming!
Christmas is coming!
Only ___ more days until Christmas!

❋ DAY 23 ❋
THE WAITING REWARD

Jesus grows up in Nazareth. Luke 2:39–52

Have you ever heard someone say, "Be patient, please," "Just a minute, please," or "Not now, just wait"?

Being patient isn't easy—especially when it's almost Christmas. Only two more days to go! Your mind swirls, darts, and dances with candy canes, Christmas carols, and cookies with sprinkles. You dream of Christmas morning stockings and packages tied up with shiny bows. Why can't today be over and Christmas hurry up?

When Jesus was a boy, He knew what it was like to want to hurry things up. Every morning He traced His letters and recited the words of the law, the Torah. Every afternoon Jesus wandered into the carpenter shop to make iron-tipped plows and stone head hammers. Every Sabbath Jesus heard the ram horn's three blasts—*toot, toot, toot!*—then walked to the synagogue.

Someday Jesus would teach; today He just listened.

Someday He'd make a blind man see; today He made tables and doors.

Someday He'd walk on water; today He walked the path to church.

Couldn't things just hurry up?

Still, every day Jesus worked hard doing everyday, ordinary, Monday-through-Friday things.

> The child [Jesus] grew and became strong; he was filled with wisdom, and the grace of God was upon him (Luke 2:40).

It's okay to dream about Christmas Day—chocolate fudge, new toys, and extra time with family. Of course you're excited for Christmas! But while you wait, be patient and work hard at everyday things.

(In the following sentences, fill in the blanks with your child's favorite things and "everyday" things.)

Someday (soon!) you'll _____ (*read the Christmas story*) but today you'll _____ (*practice piano*).

Someday (soon!) you'll eat _____ (*peanut brittle*) but today you'll eat _____ (*green beans*).

Someday (soon!) you'll _____ (*dig inside your Christmas stocking*) but today you'll _____ (*take out the garbage*).

Today be patient and do the work; tomorrow you'll get the reward. "Be strong and do not give up, for your work will be rewarded" (2 Chronicles 15:7).

:: Advent Adventure: Gelatin Reward ::

SUPPLIES: Bowl, 1 pkg. flavored gelatin, 1 c. cold water or apple juice, fruit and whipped topping (optional)

DIRECTIONS:

- Mix the gelatin according to the directions. Use cold apple juice instead of cold water if you'd like.
- Refrigerate for a few minutes.
- *Parents, after a few minutes, pull the gelatin back out and offer it to your child to eat. You're hoping, of course, that he says, "But it's not ready!" Explain that if he wants gelatin instead of gelatin soup, he has to be patient. Sometimes patience means getting a better reward.*
- Pop the mixture back into the refrigerator and wait until the gelatin sets.
- Top with fruit and whipped topping. Eat and enjoy your reward. Wasn't the wait worth it?

I WONDER

When does Christmas start? When Dad and
Mom get up or when I wake up?

PRAYER TO SHARE

Dear God, only two more days 'til Christmas! I'm so excited I
could burst. While I wait for my "tomorrow" things, remind
me to be patient and work hard at my "today" things. Amen.

CHRISTMAS COUNTDOWN

It's coming! It's coming!
Christmas is coming!
Only ___ more days until Christmas!

THE RISING SUN

Jesus brings light into the world.
ISAIAH 9:2; LUKE 1:78–79

Have you ever watched a sunrise? The sun's fingers stretch over the top of the world and darkness runs away. The sky becomes a swirl of red, orange, pink, and yellow. The red cardinal fluffs his feathers. The robin begins to chatter, hungry for his wormy breakfast. The dew begins to shimmer, then the sun appears. You blink open your eyes and s–t–r–e–t–c–h, then jump out of bed.

Everything asleep is now awake.

Singing-running-playing awake.

Eating-laughing-learning awake.

Everything dark is now light.

Shimmering-shining-sparkling light.

Bright-glowing-happy light.

The whole world comes alive!

God's Word says Jesus is like the rising sun.

The rising sun will come to us from heaven to shine on those living in darkness (Luke 1:78–79).

The sun brings light and life to our world; Jesus brings light and life to our hearts. When we sin, darkness comes into our lives. Sin creeps into our hearts. But on Christmas Day, Jesus, the Light of the world, was born. When He comes into your heart, He pours new life inside you. Everything that was dark is now light.

:: ADVENT FAMILY ACTIVITY ::

Add one last candle , the CHRIST candle, to the center of the evergreen boughs. As you light each of the five candles, remember that Jesus is why we celebrate Christmas. He is at the center of everything we do. He is the Light of the world.

I WONDER

When the sun comes up,
where does the darkness go?

PRAYER TO SHARE

Dear Jesus, You are the Light of the World. I want
to shine Your light to those around me. Amen.

CHRISTMAS COUNTDOWN

It's coming! It's coming!
Christmas is coming!
Only ___ more day until Christmas!

❄ DAY 25 ❄
COMING—AGAIN!

Jesus is coming back to earth.
ACTS 1:9–11

What are we celebrating today? *Jesus' birthday.*

What else do we celebrate at Christmas? (*Parents, instead of answering this question, step right into the devotional below.*)

Today we're celebrating Christmas, the day Jesus came to earth. But we also celebrate the day He'll come back to earth. Only this time…

- He won't be a baby but a man;
- not a carpenter's son but a King;
- not wrapped in swaddling clothes but wrapped in the clouds;
- not surrounded by shepherds and Magi but surrounded by angels;
- not accompanied by the sounds of bleating sheep but by the sounds of seven trumpets;
- Jesus will be King!

> *He [Jesus] is Lord of lords and King of kings—and with him will be his called, chosen and faithful followers* (Revelation 17:14).

Jesus will come as King and judge the earth. He'll create a new heaven and earth (Isaiah 65:17) with no crying (just laughing), no frowning (just smiling), no growling stomachs (just full tummies). Little boys and little girls will lead a lion with their hands. The wolf will walk right next to the lamb. Jesus will bring peace to earth!

Just like the people of Israel waited for Jesus' birth, just like you waited for Christmas, you can wait to celebrate the day Jesus will come back.

Name Alert

___ ___ ___ ___ of Lords and

___ ___ ___ ___ of ___ ___ ___ ___ ___

:: ADVENT ADVENTURE: JEWEL NECKLACE ::

Jesus will rule from a city with streets of gold. He'll make each gate from an enormous pearl. He'll decorate the city with twelve precious gems, including sapphire (blue), emerald (green), carnelian (red), beryl (clear), and amethyst (purple). (See Revelation 21:18–20.)

Create this necklace (or garland) to remind you of the city where those who love Jesus will live someday.

SUPPLIES: String (enough to make either a garland or a necklace), scissors, tape, toothpick, fruit-flavored Lifesavers (4 for every foot of string)

DIRECTIONS:
- Tape one end of the string to the toothpick in order to thread the string through the Lifesaver.
- Pull the toothpick through the first Lifesaver "gem" until the gem is about 4" from the end of the string.
- Loop the toothpick back through the gem.
- Add a second gem, pulling it about 3" to 4" from the first gem.
- Loop the toothpick back through the second gem.
- Continue until the necklace/garland is the length you'd like.
- Snip the toothpick and tape off. Either tie the two ends of string together to form a necklace or tie a knot around the first and last gems and drape the garland around your tree.

I WONDER

What will the best part be about Jesus coming back?

PRAYER TO SHARE

Dear Jesus, today we celebrate Your birthday. Hurray! Christmas is finally here. Thank You for coming into the world. Someday—soon, I hope—You'll come back. Then I'll celebrate again. Amen. (Based on Revelation 22:20.)

CHRISTMAS COUNTDOWN
CHRISTMAS IS HERE!

ABOUT THE AUTHOR

Carol Garborg is a parent educator, author, and speaker. She has spent fifteen years teaching and telling stories to children of various ages. She is passionate about God's Word and delights in showing families that His Word is fun, exciting, and relevant.

Carol has developed the *Faith Family-Style* curriculum and coaches families and churches on how to learn faith principles in an intergenerational setting that's packed with fun and meaning.

Carol currently lives in Minneapolis, Minnesota, with her husband and son.

For more information, go to www.faithfamilystyle.com.

SUPPLY LIST

Supplies are listed for all crafts and activities. See daily activities for more specific information.

ADVENT CANDLE ARRANGEMENT—Five candles, evergreen boughs, holly, candy canes, and pinecones.

DAY 1 — a wreath, 15 small plain ball ornaments, permanent markers (gold or silver to go with the holiday theme)

DAY 2 — Small plain gift bag, four pieces of paper that will fit inside the bag, glue stick, markers

DAY 3 — Lamp or flashlight

DAY 6 — (Opt. 1) Computer, paper, color printer; (Opt. 2) 2 c. sea salt, ½ c. water, aluminum foil, 8"x10" piece of cardboard, decorative pieces (e.g., mini pinecones, Lego people), paper, markers

DAY 7 — Deflated balloon; (Opt. 1) table covering (e.g., newspaper), pen, tree pattern (see page 132), cone-shaped coffee filter, water, scissors, colored markers, string or yarn; (Opt. 2) a squat wide-mouthed jar (like a salsa jar), light-colored wrapping paper, glue stick, tea light

DAY 8 — A magnifying glass

DAY 9 — Eight 5-oz. paper cups with waxy coating (e.g., Dixie cups), 8 Popsicle sticks, 8"x8" pan, blender, 3 c. vanilla ice cream, ¾ c. orange juice, 8 strawberries, blender

DAY 11 — 1 piece construction paper, scissors, markers (or old magazines and glue stick)

DAY 12 — 6 jumbo craft sticks, small googly eyes, miscellaneous decorations (e.g., pom-poms, cotton balls, fabric or flannel, markers, buttons)

DAY 13 — (Opt. 1) Table covering (e.g., newspaper), 4" terra cotta pot, 3" or 4" Styrofoam ball, 1 bottle of gold acrylic craft paint, paintbrush, white card stock or craft foam (roughly 9"x12"); all-purpose glue, glitter glue, angel wing pattern (see page 133), (Opt. 2) one 8½"x11" sheet of paper, scissors, pen or pencil, angel pattern (see page 134)

DAY 14 — Small jar, large jar, dish soap, food coloring

DAY 15 — *The Foot Book* by Dr. Seuss, 1 piece construction paper, washable paint, paintbrush, pencil—and a little imagination

DAY 16 — All-purpose glue, poster board, marker

DAY 17 — Flashlight

DAY 18 — Handful of sand (or salt or sugar)

DAY 19 — 2 feet of wide ribbon, 1 (8½"x11") piece of card stock, all-purpose glue, markers, old magazines, scissors

DAY 21 — Box of sugar cubes (next to the regular sugar in the grocery store), all-purpose glue, ruler, paper, pencil, paper plate

DAY 22 — Milk, chocolate chips, marshmallow creme (not marshmallow topping), vanilla, sprinkles or crushed candy canes, malted milk balls (optional)

DAY 23 — 1 pkg. flavored gelatin, 1 c. cold apple juice (optional), bananas or other fruit and whipped topping (optional)

DAY 25 — String (enough to make either a garland or a necklace), scissors, tape, toothpick, fruit-flavored Lifesavers (4 for every foot of string)

CHRISTMAS TREE ORNAMENT PATTERN
DAY 7

ANGEL WING PATTERN
DAY 13

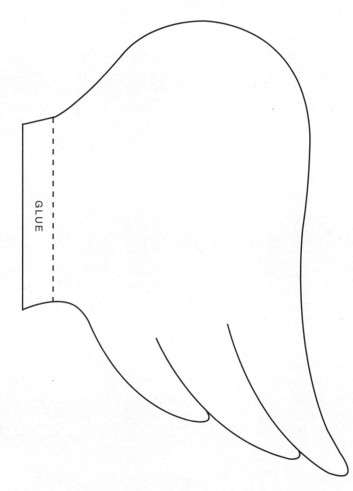

GLUE

ANGEL PATTERN
DAY 13